Have You Got it on Yet?

PETER VAN STRAATEN

FOURTH ESTATE · London

First published by De Harmonie

First published in Great Britain in 1993 by
Fourth Estate Limited
289 Westbourne Grove
London W11 2QA

A catalogue record for this book is available from the British Library

ISBN 1–85702–142–8

Printed in Great Britain by Biddles Ltd., Guildford.

"DON'T YOU THINK THAT'S RUSHING THINGS, BRIAN? WE'VE ONLY KNOWN EACH OTHER EIGHTEEN MONTHS!"

"YOU SAY THE SWEETEST THINGS,
MICHAEL. BUT YOU DO THINK I'M
A BIT TARTY TOO, DON'T YOU?"

" ON ONE CONDITION – IF IT'S
DISASTROUS, I CAN SAY SO "

"ARE YOU STILL GETTING IT REGULARLY, OLD CHAP?"

"WHY NOT COME TO MY PLACE AND LET ME SHOW YOU MY TATTOOS?"

"OH VERY WELL THEN. BUT NO YELLING!"

"COME ON, CAROL. IT'LL BE OVER IN A JIFFY"

"WELL IT HAD TO HAPPEN
SOME TIME, I HOPE YOU
KNOW WHAT TO DO"

"RIGHT.....WHO STARTS?"

"OR DO YOU WANT ANOTHER
DRINK FIRST?"

"I'M SORRY. I'VE CHANGED MY MIND"

"IS IT WORTH GETTING UNDRESSED
OR WILL THIS JUST BE ANOTHER
OF YOUR QUICKIES?"

" NOT EASY, IS IT ? "

"PLEASE KEEP IT SIMPLE
TODAY, ROBERT"

"I HOPE YOU KNOW YOUR
WAY AROUND."

"CAN WE TURN THE LIGHT OUT OR
DO YOU INSIST ON SEEING ME?"

"THAT'S IT ....TAKE IT GENTLY"

"OK, I'LL EXPLAIN ONE MORE TIME...
IT'S IN THE MIDDLE."

"AT LEAST SHOW ME HOW!"

"DON'T THINK I'M BEING LAZY,
BUT COULDN'T YOU DO IT
BETTER YOURSELF?"

" WHAT DO YOU MEAN ? "

"DO I ALWAYS HAVE TO DO
EVERYTHING MYSELF?"

"OH SORRY, AM I TALKING
TOO MUCH?"

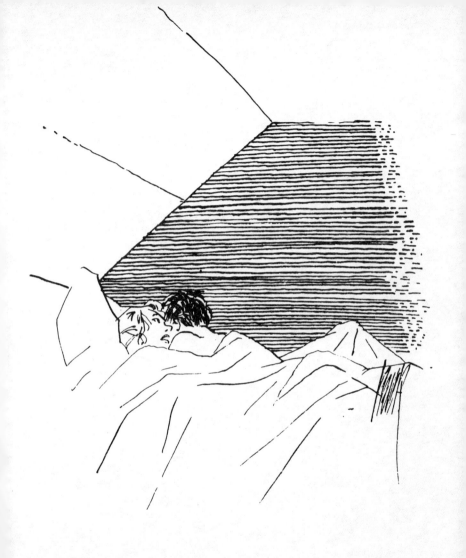

" GOSH —ARE YOU IN ALREADY?"

"OH! AAH! GLEN, CAN'T YOU TEACH THIS TO GREG?"

"GOD, YOU'RE NOISY!"

"WELL, WASN'T THAT NICE AND QUICK!"

" OH THANK GOODNESS.
HE'S STOPPED MOVING "

"NOW PUT THE LIGHT BACK ON
SO I CAN FINISH MY BOOK"

"SORRY. I WAS MILES AWAY"

"YOU WEREN'T REALLY IN THE MOOD, WERE YOU?"

"THERE. AND NOW I SUPPOSE
YOU WANT A CIGARETTE."

"I DID COME THAT TIME IN PARIS,
SO THERE'S STILL HOPE."

"I HAD A BIT OF ONE, I THINK"

"NEARLY, DARLING, NEARLY"

"NO POST-MORTEM?"

"HONESTLY BILL, IT WASN'T THAT BAD"

"DIZZY, DO YOU MIND IF I JUST
RING MY MOTHER?"

"YOU'RE RIGHT OUT OF
CONDITION, PAUL"

"RUBBISH, HE WAS HOPELESS!
YOU'RE MUCH BETTER "

"JUST WAIT TILL NEXT WEEK WHEN I GET THAT BIGGER BED!"

"IS YOUR NAME PENNY?"

"OH LOVE, PETER WAS EVEN MORE IMPOTENT"

"BUT WHAT DID _YOU_ THINK OF IT?"

"THIS BED'S DREADFUL. I BET
THAT'S WHAT'S WRONG."

"WHY DON'T YOU GO AND MAKE US
BREAKFAST INSTEAD, DARLING."

"ANN, BE HONEST— ARE YOU PHASING ME OUT?"

"SO WE WON'T BE SEEING
EACH OTHER AGAIN?"

" WISHING YOU HADN'T ? "